CAROLS FOR GROUNDHOG'S DAY

Jo A. Hiestand Books

The McLaren Mysteries
Cold Revenge
Last Seen
Shadow in the Smoke
Brushed With Injustice
An Unfolding Trap
No Known Address
An Unwilling Suspect
Arrested Flight
Photo Shoot
Empty Handed
Black Moon

The Peak District Mysteries
A Staged Murder
A Recipe For Murder
In A Wintry Wood
A Touch of Murder
The Stone Hex (by Jo A. Hiestand and Paul Hornung)
Searching Shadows (by Jo A. Hiestand and Paul Hornung)
An Old Remedy

Stand-Alone Books
Cider, Swords & Straw: Celebrating British Customs
   (cookbook with customs information and Peak District
   Mystery book synopses)
Carols for Groundhog's Day
Tea in a Tin Cup: Travels and Culinary Reminiscences of
   a Writer

WRITING AS JESSIE MCALAN
The Linn House Mysteries
The House on Devil's Bar
A Hasty Grave
A Whisper of Water

Carols

For Groundhog's Day

Jo A. Hiestand

Artwork by Christine Eisenmayer

Cover and Interior Design by Cousins House

First Printing 2013 Golden Harvest Press
ISBN 9780615861470
Second Printing 2019 Cousins House

Cousins House

Published by Cousins House

Printed in the United States of America

Dedicated to Rumple and Rusty,
the current crop

I would like to thank:
Chris, for her wonderful illustrations;
Carol & Doug, my parents,
for making me possible;
Humphrey, the first of many groundhogs
who have visited and feasted at my
back deck and who made the carols possible.

Praise for *Carols for Groundhog's Day*

"I laughed so hard over these carols I couldn't get to sleep!" - *Sleeping Beauty*

"Jo Hiestand has the magic touch. These songs are in-*genie*-ous!" - *Aladdin*

"Wonderful songs, without a shadow of a doubt!"
– *The Man in the Moon*

"This book is just right." - *Goldilocks*

"Forget the cheese! This book stands alone in its field!" - *The Farmer in the Dell*

Table of Contents

The Carols

Springtime's Here (Tune: *Good King Wenceslas*)

1. Springtime's here, the groundhog cries,
   springtime with its flowers.
   Warming sunshine certifies
   July's cauliflowers.
   So, we grab the rake and hoe,
   big bag of peat mosses.
   Nurs'ry purchases in tow
   we replace last year's losses.

2. In the mud and in the mire,
   ruthlessly we're kneeling;
   yanking brambles, pulling briars,
   no mercy we're feeling
   'til the empty ground complies
   to receive our planting.
   Never mind the snow-specked sky —
   the groundhog's dominant-ing.

3. If the ground is hard as nails
   and the water's frozen,
   wise old groundhog never fails —
   his forecast we've chosen.
   If seeds fail to germinate
   take this friendly warnin' —
   come next springtime's planting date
   stay out of the garden.

That Wise Groundhog (Tune: *We Three Kings*)

1. That wise groundhog, up from his den
    sniffing, searching, telling us when
    winter's fading, spring's elating-ly coming with the
    wren.

CHORUS:
Oh, Hog of wisdom, brainy one, tell us when the spring will
come.
No more snowing, it's de troping, and getting wearisome.

2. Pinafores and T-shirts have I,
    warmer weather garments imply
    we once wore them. To restore them soon is our
    great outcry.

    [Repeat CHORUS]

3. Sweaters comfy, mugsful of tea
    testify to winter's degrees.
    From this whacking we are cracking, this I guarantee.

    [Repeat CHORUS]

I've Been Walkin' 'Round in Sweaters
(Tune: *I've Been Workin' on the Railroad*)

I've been walkin' 'round in sweaters, fleece-lined boots also,
I've been walkin' round in sweaters just to keep me from the cold.
I have on so many layers I can barely move my arms;
It would be so nice to shed clothes and be truly warm.
For we're tired of the snow, tired of the snow, tired of the snow and sleet;
tired of the snow, tired of the snow, tired of the snow and sleet.
Oh we want an end to this weather, oh we want an end to this snow,
yes, we want an end to this freezing, and all temps of twelve below.
We want warmth!
Fee fi phooey on snow, fee fi phooey on snow, fee fi phooey on snow! Yearning for the hot sun's glow!

Oh, the Groundhog Eats (Tune: *Polly Wolly Doodle*)

1. Oh, the groundhog eats your beets and beans,
   for it's yummy in the tummy all the day.
   He will chow 'em down so he won't stay lean
   yes, it's yummy in the tummy all the day.

CHORUS:
Eating well so he'll swell, from sunrise 'til end of day
he will eat a peach or cherry, lima bean or ripe strawberry
chompin' through your veggie patch to your dismay.

2. Oh, the groundhog likes his carrots raw,
   for it's yummy in the tummy all the day.
   Nothing is too tough that he can't gnaw,
   yes, it's yummy in the tummy all the day.
[Repeat CHORUS]

3. He will eat the squash or the artichoke,
    for it's yummy in the tummy all the day.
    Your tomatters, too, as a little joke,
    yes, it's yummy in the tummy all the day.
[Repeat CHORUS]

4. He will chew the corn right off the cob,
    for it's yummy in the tummy all the day.
    No one can do a finer job,
    yes, it's yummy in the tummy all the day.
[Repeat CHORUS]

5. He will pack on pounds 'til Au-túmn declares,
    for it's yummy in the tummy all the day,
    he should hi-ber-nate in his winter lair,
    yes, it's yummy in the tummy all the day.
[Repeat CHORUS]

6. Oh, the groundhog's fur is brown and thick,
    for it's yummy in the tummy all the day.
    It will keep out cold, rain, ice and ticks,
    yes, it's yummy in the tummy all the day.
[Repeat CHORUS]

7. Oh, the groundhog is a lucky guy,
    for it's yummy in the tummy all the day.
    There's no worry 'bout his waist or thighs,
    yes, it's yummy in the tummy all the day.
[Repeat CHORUS]

On the First Day of Feasting (Tune: *The Twelve Days of Christmas*)

1. On the first day of feasting the groundhog ate with zeal
    a peach pit and all of the peel.

2. On the second day of feasting the groundhog ate with zeal
    two acorn squash, and a peach pit and all of the peel.

3. On the third day of feasting the groundhog ate with zeal
    three purple grapes, two acorn squash, and a peach pit and all of the peel.

4. On the fourth day of feasting the groundhog ate with zeal
    four juicy plums, three purple grapes, two acorn squash, and a peach pit and all of the peel.

5. On the fifth day of feasting the groundhog ate with zeal
    five lima beans! Four juicy plums, three purple grapes, two acorn squash, and a peach pit and all of the peel.

6. On the sixth day of feasting the groundhog ate with zeal
    six ripe tomatoes, five lima beans! Four juicy plums, three purple grapes, two acorn squash, and a peach pit and all of the peel.

7. On the seventh day of feasting the groundhog ate with zeal
    seven pounds of spinach, six ripe tomatoes, five lima beans! Four juicy plums, three purple grapes, two acorn squash, and a peach pit and all of the peel.

8. On the eighth day of feasting the groundhog ate with zeal
eight choc'late muffins, seven pounds of spinach, six ripe tomatoes, five lima beans! Four juicy plums, three purple grapes, two acorn squash, and a peach pit and all of the peel.

9. On the ninth day of feasting the groundhog ate with zeal
nine crisp, orange carrots, eight choc'late muffins, seven pounds of spinach, six ripe tomatoes, five lima beans! Four juicy plums, three purple grapes, two acorn squash, and a peach pit and all of the peel.

10. On the tenth day of feasting the groundhog ate with zeal
ten nuts and berries, nine crisp, orange carrots, eight choc'late muffins, seven pounds of spinach, six ripe tomatoes, five lima beans! Four juicy plums, three purple grapes, two acorn squash, and a peach pit and all of the peel.

11. On the eleventh day of feasting the groundhog ate with zeal
eleven limp zucchini, ten nuts and berries, nine crisp, orange carrots, eight choc'late muffins, seven pounds of spinach, six ripe tomatoes, five lima beans! Four juicy plums, three purple grapes, two acorn squash, and a peach pit and all of the peel.

12. On the twelfth day of feasting the groundhog ate with zeal
Twelve broken cookies, eleven limp zucchini, ten nuts and berries, nine crisp, orange carrots, eight choc'late muffins, seven pounds of spinach, six ripe tomatoes, five lima beans! Four juicy plums, three purple grapes, two acorn squash, and a peach pit and all of the peel.

New Sleeves (Tune: *Greensleeves*)

1. Alas! My clothes are wearing out from constant, non-
   stop wearing,
   the sweater's sleeve stretched out of shape, the
   trouser's knees are saggin'.

CHORUS:
New sleeves on new bought clothes, no threadbare knees, no
rips, no holes!
Joy, joy for shorts so thin, for buttons firmly fastened.

2. November through the gales of March these clothes I
   constant inhabit,
   ward off the cold with wool so old that moths no
   more can grab it.
[Repeat CHORUS]

3. Thick socks and hat, crocheted cravats and corduroy
   excessive;
   oh, Groundhog, dear, say spring is here! We'll shed
   these fabrics oppressive.
[Repeat CHORUS]

4. I long to glimpse a hint of skin, a toe or just one
   finger;
   my mem'ry of my knee grows dim, an elbow image
   does linger.
No sleeves or mittened hand, no more worn clothes I can't
withstand!
Toes flex from sandals new. The groundhog disbands winter
garments!

Should Rays of Sunshine (Tune: *Auld Lang Syne*)

1. Should rays of sunshine be forgot and never brought
    to mind?
    Should rays of sunshine be forgot through wintry
    blast unkind?
    Through wintry blast unkind, my dear, through
    wintry blast unkind,
    Should rays of sunshine be forgot through wintry
    blast unkind?

2. The sky is gray, the clouds are dark, it's been this way
    all week.
    With snow and sleet for miles around it's looking
    mighty bleak.
    It's looking mighty bleak, my dear, it's looking might
    bleak,
    With snow and sleet for miles around it's looking
    mighty bleak.

3. Snow shovels push the snow away but ice we'll have
    to blast.
    So set the dynamite and run, more snow's in the
    forecast.
    More snow's in the forecast, my dear, more snow's in
    the forecast,
    So set the dynamite and run, more snow's in the
    forecast.

4. Oh, groundhog wise, your shadow now we do not
    want to see.
    Remain and bring a sign of spring to snow-crazed
    refugees.
    To snow-crazed refuges, dear Hog, to snow-crazed
    refugees,
    through days so bleak 'tis spring we seek for snow-
    crazed refugees.

Joy (Tune: *Joy to the World*)

1. Joy to the world! The groundhog's here.
    Let winter's bonds be broke.
    Let every voice be raised in cheer
    with budding of the oak, with budding of the oak,
    with budding, with budding of the oak.

2. Joy to the world, the shadow's hid,
    six weeks we'll soon have spring.
    From ice, sleet and snow we'll all be rid
    of winter's offering, of winter's offering,
    of winter's, of winter's offering.

We'll Be Nappin' In Our Hammocks
(Tune: *She'll Be Comin' Round the Mountain*)

1. We'll be wearin' thick wool sweaters if he runs,
   We'll be wearin' thick wool sweaters if he runs,
   We'll be wearin' thick wool sweaters,
   We'll be wearin' thick wool sweaters,
   We'll be wearin' thick wool sweaters if he runs.

2. We'll be loungin' in our swim suits if he stays,
   We'll be loungin' in our swim suits if he stays,
   We'll be loungin' in our swim suits, We'll be loungin'
   in our swim suits,
   We'll be loungin' in our swim suits if he stays.

3. We'll be guzzlin' rich hot choc'late if he runs,
   We'll be guzzlin' rich hot choc'late if he runs,
   We'll be guzzlin' rich hot choc'late, We'll be guzzlin'
   rich hot choc'late,
   We'll be guzzlin' rich hot choc'late if he runs.

4. We'll be downin' quarts of ice cream if he stays,
   We'll be downin' quarts of ice cream if he stays,
   We'll be downin' quarts of ice cream, We'll be
   downin' quarts of ice cream,
   We'll be downin' quarts of ice cream if he stays.

5. We'll be sleepin' under blankets if he runs,
   We'll be sleepin' under blankets if he runs,
   We'll be sleepin' under blankets, We'll be sleepin'
   under blankets,
   We'll be sleepin' under blankets if he runs.

6. We'll be nappin' in our hammocks if he stays,
   We'll be nappin' in our hammocks if he stays,
   We'll be nappin' in our hammocks, We'll be nappin'
   in our hammocks,
   We'll be nappin' in our hammocks if he stays.

Home Underground (Tune: *Home On the Range*)

1. O give him a home where the winds never moan, and
    the snow merely flies past the door.
    In his warm wintry den he is dreaming of when he
    can eat and your garden explore.
CHORUS:
Home, home underground in his den that keeps winter at bay.
Dreaming dreams of fine meals with vegetarian appeals,
growing fresh in your garden each day.

2. Half the year he will sleep in his den buried deep
    in the ground of a field or your home.
    It's delightful when food is nearby and it's good,
    making certain he never will roam.
[Repeat CHORUS]

3. His den he will leave at the hint of a breeze
    smelling warm with the freshness of spring.
    He is lean and he's brown, having lost many pounds,
    so he's eager to start breakfasting.
[Repeat CHORUS]

4. He will eat all your flow'rs in the space of an hour,
   giving pref'rence to those that cost more.
   He will chew on your rose, to your weeds thumb his
   nose, your choice kumquats he'll truly adore.
[Repeat CHORUS]

Lonesome Row (Tune: *Lonesome Road*)

1. Look down, look down that lonesome row
   where no more veggies grow.
   The plants, once lush, are shorn and trampled,
   mere stubs to weed and hoe.

2. No fruits, no leaves, the stems are barren
   just like a short flagpole.
   A second crop awaits the gnawing
   of groundhog, hare and vole.

Cabin Fever (Tune: *Angels We Have Heard on High*)

1. Cabin fever's hold is stout,
    Sanity needs great repair.
    Sun's been hidden for too long,
    Wish the cold would go elsewhere.

CHORUS:
Oh – groundhog! Show us springtime's gladness.
Oh – groundhog! Free us from this madness.

2. With the onslaught of the ice
    Rental movies all checked out.
    I've read every book here twice,
    Dusted, replaced bathroom grout!
[Repeat CHORUS]

3. Sixteen windows, twenty doors,
    I have counted everyone.
    Washed and waxed the sills and floors,
    and the crosswords all are done.
[Repeat CHORUS]

Down in the Southland (Tune: *Down in the Valley*)

1. Down in the southland, southland so low
    where there is sunshine instead of snow.
    Instead of snow, dear, instead of snow,
    only green grasses instead of snow.

2. Staring at whiteness, it lays all around,
    nothing but snowdrifts cover the ground.
    Cover the ground, dear, cover the ground,
    tired of snowflakes that cover the ground.

3. Ads for Jamaica tell of warm breeze,
    sun-drenched blue waters that never will freeze.
    Never will freeze, dear, never will freeze,
    in sun-drenched Jamaica *I* never will freeze!

4. Can't wait for Groundhog, get me a seat,
    fly me down south for my share of the heat.
    Share of the heat, dear, share of the heat,
    wallow in sunshine, my share of the heat.

Groundhogs are More than a 'Day'

Most people know the old weather saw about the groundhog and February 2. Spring's early appearance depends on him not seeing his shadow (a shadow forecasts six more weeks of winter, so he scurries back into his underground burrow; an overcast day produces no shadow, so he stays topside to await Spring's arrival).

Well, this shadow thing is fun, but how did it all start? It goes back a long way...

How it came to be

Groundhog's Day began in the 18th and 19th centuries as a Pennsylvania German custom in southeastern and central Pennsylvania. It's rooted in ancient European weather lore, a badger or sacred bear taking the forecaster role instead of a groundhog. The holiday also has ties to the medieval Catholic holiday of Candlemas—also known as the Purification of the Virgin, or the Presentation—as well as to the Pagan festival of Imbolc, the seasonal turning point of the Celtic calendar, which is celebrated on February 1. Imbolc also involves weather prognostication.

In America, a reference to Groundhog Day can be found as early as February 5, 1841 in a diary entry. Storekeeper James Morris, of Berks County, Pennsylvania states:

"Last Tuesday, the 2nd, was Candlemas day, the day on which, according to the Germans, the Groundhog peeps out of his winter quarters and if he sees his shadow he pops back for another six weeks nap, but if the day be cloudy he remains out, as the weather is to be moderate."

A Scottish poem might also be the source for the day in the US:

As the light grows longer
The cold grows stronger
If Candlemas be fair and bright
Winter will have another flight
If Candlemas be cloud and snow
Winter will be gone and not come again
A farmer should on Candlemas day
Have half his corn and half his hay
On Candlemas day if thorns hang a drop
You can be sure of a good pea crop

But there are other interesting 'fun facts' you may not know about this interesting mammal.

Did You Know...

- The groundhog measures from approximately 20 to 35 inches long. Color of hair varies from grizzle grayish brown with a reddish or yellowish cast, to darker brown. The belly is light buff to white. The tail is dark brown to black.

- Groundhogs molt once a year, May through September. The molt begins simultaneously at the face and tail, working backward and forward to meet in the animal's middle.

- During hibernation, a groundhog loses one-third to one-half their weight they had in the autumn.

- Like beavers and other gnawing rodents, groundhog incisors grow constantly, so they must be used persistently to wear them down.

- When alarmed, the groundhog emits a loud, shrill whistle. When angry, their teeth chatter and a muffled bark is given. When fighting, they squeal or growl loudly.

- Den sites are usually in open land bordered by timber, along fencerows or stream banks.

- A burrow system may be comprised of several entrances, tunnels and chambers. The main entrance to the burrow is frequently beside a tree stump or rock. A mound of earth excavated from the burrow is at the main entrance, serving as an observation deck, sunning spot and latrine.

- Groundhogs usually hibernate by the end of October or mid-November, although the oldest and fattest adults hibernate first.

- Male groundhogs emerge from hibernation and sometimes roam about on moonlit nights to search for mates.

- Groundhogs have been known to burrow out 716 pounds of soil when digging their dens.

- Groundhogs can swim and climb trees.

- Daily food consumption is as much as 1 ½ pounds, which is remarkable, considering the average weight of an adult is 4 ½ to 9 pounds. Some individuals, though, have attained a weight of 30 pounds!

- In the spring, groundhogs seek the salt spread on roads during winter snow removal. Salt is essential to their diet.

- Groundhog range is from southern Arkansas, north to Ontario, then west to the Pacific and up into Alaska. Its range eastward includes Missouri to the

Atlantic   seaboard   and   up   into   mainland Newfoundland.

- Daily activities outside the burrow are eating and lying in the sun.

- Occasionally groundhogs climb trees to eat leaves, apples and papaws.

Celebrate with a Groundhog Day Party!

W hat a great excuse for a party! And a perfect time! Christmas, Hanukkah and New Year's Eve are over, a large portion of winter is still in the offing, and the Winter Blahs are upon us. It's time for some fun!

Since Groundhog Day deals with forecasting the weather, your party should center on forecasts—personal as well as weather-related. You can be as silly or as serious as you wish, of course, but the theme all starts with the invitation.

Invitation Suggestion

Here's an easy idea for a mailed invitation. Cut colored card stock into quarters. Cut out snowflakes or flowers from a magazine or wrapping paper and paste one of them on the card stock quarter. You can wrap them around the edge of the card, as shown below, or paste the entire graphic onto your card. Hand write the party information onto the card. Graphics are obtainable off the Internet, too; find some you like and print them out. You can create an invitation on the computer—in which case, print it out before you paste your graphic onto the paper.

February 2nd — sun or fog —
that's the day for the groundhog.
Snow on the tree stump,
robin on the wing
tells of winter or of spring.
Jump in your car—rain or shine
we'll have fun, games and we'll dine!
Celebrate Groundhog's Day!
DAY _____
DATE _____
TIME _____
PLACE _____
RSVP (your phone number) _____

Decorations

According to folklore, the event predicts the arrival of spring. Will winter remain for six more weeks or will flowers pop forth quite soon from the earth? You can illustrate this prediction in your table centerpiece. If you have a chandelier above your table, hang snowflakes by thread, fishing line or thin string from the light fixture. Measurements of the string should vary so that your snowflakes dangle at different lengths. There are several types of snowflakes on the market: white crocheted, red wooden, silver paper.... Or cut your own from folded pieces of paper.

Tools Needed:
- Paper (must be a square piece).
- Scissors

Instructions:

1 Cut a piece of paper into a square shape.

2 Fold the square in half diagonally. You now have a triangle shape.

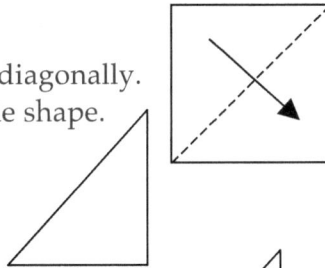

3 Fold the triangle in half diagonally.

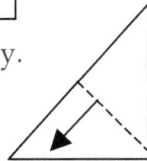

4 Fold the triangle into thirds so that it becomes a long, narrow shape,

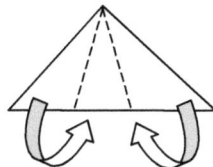

with one side folded to the front, the other side folded to the back.
Make sure that the outer edges line up with the folded edges.

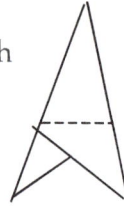

5 Trim the extra flaps of paper off the end of your triangle, so it ends up in a cone shape.

6 Around the outside of the triangle, cut some shapes: circles, squares, triangles, curves...

7 Unfold the paper to reveal your snowflake.

A large vase of flowers should sit below the hanging snowflakes. This creates the two sides of the groundhog's forecast: winter and spring. This arrangement is especially good if you are having a buffet and the table holds the buffet food. If you are having a sit down tea or meal, you might want to have small vases of several flowers at each place setting.

White dishes are especially good, serving as the 'winter' element. Conversely, any floral pattern dishes would also be fine.

If you don't have snowflakes or are allergic to flowers, you could hang mittens from the chandelier and have a vase of silk flowers below it, or fill new terra cotta flowerpots with a mixture of plastic or metal icicles and small hand garden tools such as a trowel, garden gloves and a hand rake. Or fill a small basket with packets of flower seeds, flower catalogs (tied into a cylinder with a ribbon is nice) and sunglasses.

If you are having a sit down meal, packets of flower seeds at each place setting are a nice take-home gift for your guests.

Just let your imagination soar—anything that depicts the contrast of winter and spring would be appropriate.

Food

Serve whatever you like that fits the occasion: a formal tea, a lunch or dinner, or a dessert buffet. You could serve hot and cold dishes that are associated with heavier winter and lighter spring meals, but I prefer food that fits the meal—scones, tea cakes, small sandwiches and fruit salad for a tea; heartier fare like chili, soup or stew, biscuits or gourmet sandwiches for a wintry supper.

A cake in the shape of a groundhog or merely decorated for the Big Day makes a nice dessert. You could take the opposite choice, though, and serve something lighter that evokes association with spring and summer. Ice cream, popsicles or puff pastry filled with fruit are good choices.

If you'd like to mix and match foods, keeping some fare in the lighter mode for spring and something heavier for winter, perhaps serve hot cocoa and lemonade as an interesting choice.

Something that might be fun to serve.... On a day that venerates the groundhog, you certainly wouldn't want to serve groundhog meat. So serve ground hog meat instead. In other words, pork sausage! Sausage rolls are good and especially easy to prepare and eat if you're having a buffet.

Suggested Menu for a Buffet

Sausage rolls, fruit scones, fruit tartlets, lemon pizzazz muffins, pizza muffins, corn chowder, Mexican deviled eggs, broccoli cheese log, Brussels sprouts and chicken stir fry, sweet-sour meatballs, cheery cherry cookies, Fudge Pocket cake. Lemonade and hot cocoa.

Sausage Rolls

It's not really groundhog meat —but ground hog meat will still cause a bit of amusement!

1 14x11" sheet frozen puff pastry
½ pound bulk pork sausage
1 egg

Grease a large cookie sheet and set aside. Place 1 sheet of frozen puff pastry, thawed but still cold, on a lightly floured surface. With a sharp knife, cut pastry lengthwise into 2 14"x5" strips. Divide pork sausage into two portions.

On a floured surface, roll each portion with your hands to make a 14" long rope. Place one sausage rope on each pastry strip. Fold the pastry over to envelope the meat. Moisten the edges of the pastry with water and press to seal closed. Cut each roll crosswise into seven 2" rolls. Cut two small diagonal slits on top of each roll. Place the rolls seam-side down on the cookie sheet. Refrigerate for 15 minutes.

Meanwhile, preheat the oven to 450° F. Brush the rolls with 1 beaten egg.

Bake about 30 minutes or until the pastry is crisp and golden and the sausage is cooked. Transfer the rolls to a wire rack to cool.

Serve warm or cold. Makes 14 rolls.

Scones are very similar to American biscuits. Though they don't keep well the second day, they are heaven to eat the day they are baked. Come to think of it, I've never had any leftovers for the second day....

Fruit Scones
2 ½ cups flour
2 tsp baking powder
1 tsp baking soda
½ tsp salt
½ cup sugar
5 TBS cold butter
1/2 cup raisins
1 egg
8-oz carton plain yogurt
grated peel of ½ lemon
milk
butter

Preheat oven to 425° F. Lightly grease a large cookie sheet and set aside. In a large bowl, sift flour, baking powder, baking soda and sale. Using your fingers, rub in the butter, cut into small pieces, until the mixture is crumbly. Mix in raisins. With a fork, stir in the egg, yogurt and lemon peel. Blend well to make a dough that barely holds together.

Turn out onto a floured surface and roll out with a floured rolling pin, making a round ½" thick. Cut into rounds with a 1 ½" cookie cutter. Place 1 to 1 ½" apart on the cookie sheet. Brush the tops of the scones lightly with milk.

Bake 10 to 12 minutes or until the scones are well risen and golden. Transfer to a wire rack to cool 5 minutes.

Split open and serve warm with butter. Makes about 18 scones.

Fruit Tartlets

Fruit evokes feelings and visions of spring....

Puff pastry shells or bake your own shells using pie
    crust in tartlet or muffin pans

Fresh or canned fruit such as strawberries,
    raspberries, blueberries, cherries, peaches, kiwi,
    mandarin orange

½ cup apricot, apple, raspberry **or** red currant jelly

Thaw the prepared puff pastry shells or bake and
completely cool your piecrust tartlets. Arrange fruit
attractively in the shells. In a small saucepan, stir the
jelly over low heat just until it is melted. Using a pastry
brush, glaze the fruit completely with the jelly. Cool
before serving.

Lemon Pizzazz Muffins

The lemony pizzazz of these muffins hints 'spring.'

Muffins:

1 ¾ cups flour

¾ cup sugar

1 TBSP grated lemon peel

1 tsp baking powder

¾ tsp baking soda

8 oz lemon yogurt

6 TBSP margarine – melted and cooled

1 egg – room temperature

1 TBSP lemon juice

Glaze:
1/3 cup lemon juice
¼ cup sugar
2 tsp grated lemon peel

Combine the glaze ingredients in a saucepan and cook over low heat, swirling the pan frequently until the sugar dissolves.

For muffins: Preheat the oven to 400° F. Spray muffin tins with non-stick oil or line cups with muffin papers. In a large bowl, mix the flour, sugar, lemon peel, baking powder, and baking soda. Make a well in the center of the ingredients. In a smaller bowl, mix the yogurt, melted and cooled margarine, egg, and 1 TBSP lemon juice. Add to the dry ingredients and stir *just* until blended (over-stirring will make your muffins tough). Spoon batter into the muffin cups and bake for approximately 20 minutes. Cool five minutes in the pan, then transfer the muffins to a wire rack. Using a wooden skewer, pierce 6 to 8 holes in each muffin top. Drizzle the hot glaze over each muffin top, coating them well. Serve the muffins at room temperature.

[**NOTE:** For a buffet, I like to serve mini muffins. Your guests can sample the muffin without having to take a larger one and they can always come back for seconds! Bake mini muffins in mini muffin trays for 10 minutes at 400° F]

Pizza Muffins

Okay, I know....groundhogs don't eat pizza. But they absolutely love tomatoes, which are in this recipe. And, given that all of 'my' groundhogs eat cookies, graham crackers, donuts and bread, they just might eat these muffins...if I ever have any left over to give them....

> 2 cups flour
> ¼ cup grated Parmesan cheese
> 1 TBSP sugar
> 2 tsp baking powder
> ¼ tsp baking soda
> ¼ tsp cayenne pepper
> ¼ cup minced tomatoes
> 1 medium garlic-crushed
> 1/2 tsp oregano
> 2 eggs – room temperature
> ¼ cup olive oil
> 1/3 cup milk
> 1/3 cup sour cream

Preheat oven to 400° F. In a large bowl, mix the flour, Parmesan cheese, sugar, baking powder, baking soda and cayenne pepper. Add the garlic and oregano. Make a well in the center of the dry ingredients and set aside. In a small bowl, mix together the tomatoes, eggs, olive oil, milk and sour cream. Pour into the dry ingredients and blend *just* until blended. Spoon batter into muffin cups lining a muffin pan.

Bake for 20-25 minutes. Cool five minutes in the pan, then turn out onto a wire rack to cool completely.

Makes 12 muffins.

Corn Chowder

Corn is a favorite groundhog food. They easily chew the kernels from the cob.

1 15-0z can cream of potato soup
1 cup light cream (or half-and-half)
1 cup milk
dash of pepper
1 15-oz can whole kernel corn – drained
1 15-oz can cream style corn

Mix all ingredients in a saucepan. Heat thoroughly. Serve with a dash of nutmeg atop each serving.

Mexican Deviled Eggs

8 hard-boiled eggs
½ cup grated cheddar cheese
¼ cup mayonnaise
¼ cup salsa – medium-hot to hot
1 TSP sour cream
pepper

Cut the hard boiled eggs in half lengthwise. In a bowl, combine the egg yolks and the remainder of the ingredients. Fill the indentations in the egg whites with the yolk mixture. Makes 16 halves.

Broccoli Cheese Log

Broccoli is a groundhog favorite. They eat it sitting upright, holding the stalk of broccoli in their paws, as though they were carrying a bouquet of flowers!

¾ pound broccoli
1 large garlic clove, minced
2 scallions, finely chopped
12 oz cream cheese
¾ cup feta cheese, crumbled
1 TBSP minced fresh dill
carrots or radishes for garnish

Using a sharp knife, cut away the very tops of the broccoli flowers so that the pieces resemble green crumbs or tiny buds. Finely chop the remaining broccoli. The flower buds should equal ¾ cup and the chopped broccoli should equal 2 cups. Set aside the buds. Steam the chopped broccoli until bright green and tender crisp 2-3 minutes. Plunge into cold water and drain well.

In a food processor or mixing bowl, combine the garlic, scallions, cream cheese, feta and dill. Process until well blended. Mix in the chopped broccoli and chill the cheese until firm, about 2 hours. Shape the cheese into a log, pressing the broccoli buds into the surface so it is covered all over.

Garnish with carrot matchsticks or radishes. Serve with crackers or raw vegetables.

Brussels Sprouts and Chicken Stir Fry

Some of 'my' groundhogs like Brussels sprouts; some do not.   But it's a veggie and, as such, may be on many groundhogs' menu.

2 TBSP peanut oil
2 garlic cloves, minced
4 cups quartered Brussels sprouts
½ cup chicken broth
1 ½ cups shredded carrots
2 boneless chicken breasts, diced
½ cup minced onions
½ tsp grated ginger
½ cup cashews

Heat 1 tablespoon of the peanut oil in a wok until very hot. Add the garlic and Brussels sprouts and stir fry to coat. Add the chicken broth and the carrots and stir-fry for 2 minutes.   Cover and steam for 1 minute. Remove the vegetables to a warmed bowl and set aside.

Heat the remaining 1 tablespoon of oil in the wok and stir fry the chicken until it is almost cooked. Add the onion and ginger and continue to stir-fry until the chicken is just done. Return the vegetables to the wok and stir fry long enough to heat through.   Add the cashews. Keep warm in a chaffing dish for your buffet.

Good served with steamed rice.

Sweet-Sour Meatballs

Another use of ground hog meat!

2 pounds bulk pork sausage
1 cup pineapple juice (*saved from the cans of
     pineapple*)
1 cup lemon juice
1/3 cup brown sugar – firmly packed
2 TBSP soy sauce
1 tsp grated ginger
2 TBSP lemon juice
2 TBSP cornstarch
2 2-oz cans chunk pineapple
2 medium green peppers

In a large skillet, brown the sausage that is rolled
into 1 ½-diameter balls. Drain well. Meanwhile, in a
bowl, combine the pineapple juice, 1 cup of lemon juice,
brown sugar, soy sauce and ginger. In a small cup,
combine and stir together the 2 TBSP of lemon juice and
the cornstarch. Set aside. Add the remaining lemon-
pineapple liquid mixture to the skillet.

Cover and simmer 20 to 25 minutes. Add the
drained pineapple chunks and the green peppers, cut
into pieces. Gradually stir in the cornstarch mixture.
Boil and stir 1 minute.

Turn into a serving dish and place over a warmer.
Yields approximately 8 dozen meatballs.

Zucchini Bites

Any gardener can tell you how much groundhogs love veggies...

½ small onion-chopped
1 clove garlic-minced
1 ½ cup (2 small) zucchini
3 eggs
6 oz Monterey Jack cheese
3 TBSP yellow cornmeal
¼ tsp cumin
¼ tsp oregano

Preheat oven to 325° F. In a large skillet, cook the onion and garlic. Cook until the onion is translucent. Add 1 12 cup grated zucchini. Cook until al dente stage. Mix together the eggs, Monterey Jack, cornmeal and spices. Mix in the zucchini. Spoon 1 tablespoon into mini muffin pans that have been greased.

Bake 15 to 18 minutes, until the eggs are set. Makes 36 appetizers.

Cheery Cherry Cookies
Cookies
2 2/3 cups flour
¼ tsp salt
1 cup powdered sugar
1 cup butter –softened
1/3 cup (1 small) banana
½ tsp vanilla extract
½ cup chopped almonds

Cherry Filling
3 oz cream cheese
1 cup powdered sugar
2 TBSP chopped maraschino cherries

To make cookies: Preheat oven to 350° F. In a large bowl, combine all ingredients. Chill the dough for easier handling. Shape the dough into wall-sized balls. Place on ungreased cookie sheets. Flatten each ball with the bottom of a drinking glass dipped in sugar. Bake for 10 to 12 minutes. Cool. Place the flat sides of two cookies together with the cherry filling, sandwich-style. Makes 36 sandwich cookies

To make filling: Soften the cream cheese in a small bowl. Blend in the powdered sugar and the chopped cherries.

[NOTE: Cookies will be crisp if you keep the filling in the refrigerator and assemble the cookies just before serving.]

Dark and White Chocolate Lemon Scones – 8 scones

You can make these small, especially if you have a scone pan that's scored into small triangular sections for the dough. I love this recipe for its flavor, but it's also nice for the party because the dark and white chocolate signify the light and shadow of The Day, and the lemon speaks of springtime.

2 cups flour
2 tbsp sugar
1 tbsp baking powder
grated zest of 2 lemons
¼ tsp salt
4 tbsp cold unsalted butter, cut into pieces
¼ cup bittersweet chocolate chips
¼ cup white chocolate chips
2 eggs
½ cup heavy cream
½ tsp cinnamon mixed with 2 tbsp sugar for
    topping, optional

Preheat oven to 400°F. In a medium bowl, combine the flour, sugar, baking powder, lemon zest and salt. Cut in the butter until the mixture resembles coarse crumbs.

Add both varieties of the chocolate chips.

In a small bowl, whisk together the eggs and cream. Add to the dry mixture and stir until a sticky dough is formed.

Turn out onto a lightly floured surface and knead gently just until the dough holds together, about 6 times. Divide into 3 equal portions and pat each into a 1-inch-thick round about 6 inches in diameter. With a knife, cut each round into quarters, making 4 wedges. The scones can also be formed by cutting out with a 3-inch cookie cutter to make 10 to 12 smaller scones.

Place the scones about 1 inch apart on a greased cookie sheet. Sprinkle the tops with the cinnamon sugar, if desired. Bake until crusty and golden brown, 15-20 minutes. Serve immediately with butter and jam.

Chocolate Cherry and Almond Toffee Apples

Okay, I know. Groundhogs don't eat chocolate or toffee. But they do love cherries and apples, so I won't apologize for including this recipe! Anyway, toffee apples are great party foods—eaten without utensils. You can use smaller apples, which would be perfect for your buffet menu. These are a jazzed up version of the humble toffee apple. Apples are coated in hot toffee, rolled in flaked almonds and dried cherries, then drizzled with dark chocolate. Enjoy!

6 Granny Smith apples
6 lollipop or popsicle sticks
1 cup semisweet chocolate chips
1 ¾ cup toffees, unwrapped
2 tablespoons water
1/2 teaspoon vanilla extract
1 ¼ cup dried cherries
½ cup flaked almonds

Insert wooden sticks 3/4 of the way into the stem end of each apple. Place apples on a baking tray covered with lightly greased aluminum foil. Place the chocolate chips into a microwave-safe bowl. Heat in the microwave at 30 second intervals, stirring between each until chocolate is melted and smooth. Set aside. Combine toffees and water in a saucepan over low heat. Cook, stirring often, until toffee melts and is smooth. Stir in the vanilla. Dip each apple into the molten toffee and gently run apples around insides of saucepan to scrape off some of the toffee. Scrape excess toffee from the apple bottoms using the side of the saucepan. Roll apples in mixture of cherries and almonds. Place on the foil. Use a spoon to drizzle chocolate over the apples. If the chocolate is too thick, thin by mixing with a little vegetable oil. Chill until ready to serve.

Dilly Cheese Truffles   +/- 3 ½ dozen appetizers

Yes, I realize groundhogs don't eat cheese, but these are wonderful snacking/buffet food, so I'm including them for your party menu idea.

9 oz cream cheese, softened
1 oz Swiss cheese, finely shredded
1 ½ tsp dried dill weed
1 tbsp lemon pepper
¼ tsp garlic powder
assorted garnish, such as minced fresh parsley,
    toasted sesame seeds, finely chopped pecans,
    chopped chives…

In a medium sized bowl, combine the cheese, dill, lemon pepper and garlic powder. Mix well and shape into one-inch sized balls.

Roll them in your choice of the garnishes, being sure to coat the entire cheese ball.

Place on tray or in baking pan and refrigerate until the cheese balls are well chilled. To serve, place them on a serving tray or put into miniature muffin/candy paper cups.

Chocolate Swirl Cheesecake

What a great dessert to serve! The chocolate swirls in this cheesecake could symbolize the winter/spring aspects of The Day. Place the serving plate on top of a bed of ice cubes to keep the cheesecake cold.

Crust:
1 cup finely crushed vanilla wagers, about 30
¼ cup sugar
¼ cup melted butter

Filling:
12 oz cream cheese, softened
2 eggs
½ cup sugar
1 tsp vanilla
2 oz semisweet chocolate

Preheat oven to 350°F. For the crust: combine the vanilla wafer crumbs, sugar and melted butter. Mix and press over bottom and 1 ½" up the side of a 8 or 9" springform pan. Bake the crust 6 minutes, or till golden brown.

To make filling: beat till creamy the cream cheese, eggs, sugar and vanilla. Melt over hot water the semisweet chocolate. Pour the cream cheese filling into the baked crust. Drizzle the melted chocolate over the filling. With a fork, gently swirl the chocolate into the cheese mixture. Bake 20 minutes or till the outer edge is set but the center is not quite firm. Cool, then serve.

Fudge Pocket Cake

A great cake that could double as a centerpiece for your table. The ring cake's hollow middle serves as a "groundhog hole." Add a picture of a groundhog coming out of the cake's center and some big plastic snowflakes alternating with silk, paper cutout, or plastic flowers.... I especially like chocolate cake for this, for it looks kind of "earthy." But a lemon cake is good, too, drizzled with cream cheese icing.

Fudge Pocket:
¾ cup sweetened condensed milk
3 oz cream cheese
6 oz semi-sweet chocolate chips
1 cup chopped nuts

Cake:
4 oz German sweet chocolate (or 4 oz semi-sweet chocolate)
2 TBSP water
2 2/3 cup flour
1 ½ cups sugar
2 tsp baking powder
½ tsp baking soda
½ tsp salt
1 cup dairy sour cream
½ cup butter – softened
1/3 cup water
1 tsp vanilla
3 eggs

Preheat oven to 350° F (325° F for a colored fluted tube pan). In a heavy saucepan, over low heat, blend the condensed milk, cream cheese and chocolate chips until the chocolate melts. Stir in the nuts. Cool for 15 minutes.

Using solid shortening or margarine (not cooking oil), grease and flour a 12-cup fluted tube pan (even a non-stick variety). In a small saucepan, over low heat, melt the German or semi-sweet chocolate in the water. In a large mixing bowl, blend the chocolate water mixture and the remaining cake ingredients —not the pocket ingredients. Beat well. Pour 4 cups cake batter into the prepared pan. Spoon the cooled pocket filling over the batter, being careful not to touch the sides of the pan. Cover the filling with the remaining batter. Bake 50 to 65 minutes or until the top springs back when lightly touched in the center. Cool upright in the pan 45 minutes. Turn onto a serving plate. Cool completely. Refrigerate. Just before serving, dust the top of the cake lightly with powdered sugar.

[**HIGH ALTITUDE NOTE:** Make the cake using 1 ¼ cups plus 1 TBSP sugar and 1 ½ tsp baking powder. Bake at 375° for 45 to 50 minutes.]

Chocolate Raspberry Brownies

6 oz unsweetened chocolate
1 cup butter
2 cups sugar
4 eggs
2 tsp vanilla extract
1 ½ cups flour
½ tsp baking powder
1 cup slivered almonds
1 cup chocolate chips
¾ cup seedless raspberry jelly

Preheat oven to 350° F. In a saucepan, melt the unsweetened chocolate and butter. Beat in the sugar, eggs and vanilla with a wire whisk. Cool slightly. Gradually stir in the flour and baking powder, stirring just until combined. Fold in the almonds and chocolate chips. Spread ¾ of the batter into a greased 13x9" pan. Smooth the raspberry jelly evenly over the top (melting the jelly in the microwave helps it spread easier.) Drop teaspoonfuls of the remaining batter on top of the jelly. Bake for 20-25 minutes. Cool and cut into bars.

Apple Cider Tea—8 servings

    2 ½ tsp black tealeaves
    2 ½ cups boiling water
    ¼ cup sugar
    ± 1 cup juice of 2 oranges
    ½ cup brandy
    5 cups apple cider, chilled
    8 thin lemon slices

Brew tea from the tealeaves and boiling water. Steep for five minutes. Place the sugar in a large bowl or pitcher. Strain the hot tea into the bowl and stir until the sugar is dissolved. Stir in the orange juice. Set aside to cool. Just before serving, stir in brandy and cider. Pour into glasses and float a lemon slice on each serving.

Minty Hot Cocoa

    1 ½ cups water
    ½ cup unsweetened cocoa powder
    1/8 tsp salt
    ½ cup sugar
    ½ tsp cinnamon
    6 cups milk
    1 ½ tsp vanilla extract
    candy canes
    marshmallows

Bring the water to a boil in a small heavy saucepan and remove from the heat. Stir in the cocoa powder, salt, sugar and cinnamon. Place over low heat and simmer gently just until the mixture has reached a slightly syrupy consistency, about two to three minutes. In a separate saucepan, heat the milk over low heat until just below the simmering point. Remove from the heat and stir in the cocoa mixture. Stir in the vanilla, then cover and let stand for five minutes before serving. Ladle the cocoa into mugs and garnish each with a candy cane or a marshmallow.

Party Time Ice Cream Soda—8 servings
1 ½ cups boiling water
6 tea bags
¼ cup sugar
3 cups apple juice, chilled
3 cups ginger ale, chilled
butter pecan, pistachio or ice cream of your choice

Pour water over the tea bags. Steep for 5 minutes. Remove the tea bags. Stir in the sugar. Cool. In large pitcher, combine tea and juice. Just before serving, add the ginger ale and top with one scoop of ice cream.

Cider Citrus Punch — 24 ½ cup servings
2 qt (8 cups) apple cider or juice, chilled
6-oz can lemonade concentrate, thawed—do not make into lemonade!
28-oz bottle ginger ale, chilled
apple or lemon slices
ice cubes or an ice mold

In a punch bowl or large pitcher, combine the cider and the concentrate. Stir well to dissolve the concentrate completely. Just before serving, add the ginger ale. If desired, garnish with the fruit slices. Serve over ice in glasses or float the ice mold in the punch bowl.

Berry Blast Smoothie—3-5 serving
1 cup apple juice
1 ½ cups lemonade
1 cup frozen raspberries
½ cup frozen strawberries
1 cup raspberry sherbet

Pour all liquid ingredients into a smoothie maker or into a food blender. Add all frozen ingredients. Blend at low setting for 30 seconds, then blend at high setting until smooth. Serve immediately.

Entertainment

Groundhog Day is a time to forecast the weather, certainly, but why not also have fun with other forecasts? You could hire a professional psychic or fortuneteller to tell guests' fortunes. If this is too costly, have a friend dress up as a fortuneteller—this seems more authentic for the episode if she is someone your guests don't know. Tell her a bit about each person who is attending. At the party, have your fortuneteller seated in a separate room. As each person comes into the room, have that person state his name so the fortuneteller will know what to say. Of course, this takes a lot of preparation on your part as host and on the friend who's playing the role. If you'd rather forego the preparation, and if your friend is good at adlibbing she can just say some outlandish, funny things to each person consulting her.

When you invite your guests, either by mailed invitation or phone call, tell them to wear socks, but don't explain why. During the party, sit everyone in a central location and read the 'Sock Fortunes' aloud. The guests' sock color forecast is always a funny part of the party.

Sock Fortunes

If new socks are gray, 'tis a year of special days.
If new socks are white, 'tis a year of delight.
If new socks are red, you'll find yourself wed.
If new socks are blue, you'll find one to woo.
If new socks are green, your year is routine.
If new socks are yellow, your year will be mellow.
If new socks are brown, 'tis a year of renown.
If new socks are cranberry, your year will be merry.
If new socks are black, for a trip you will pack.
If new socks have stripes, you'll find your true type.
If new socks are beige, you won't look your age
If new socks are orange, save them for Hallowe'en.

Pin the Tail

You can always 'pin the tail on the groundhog.' Use the graphic below or print one from the Internet. If you use this one, scan it on your computer or take it to a copy center to print into a large size such as 18x24". Scan and print out as many tails as you have guests. Of course, if the groundhog photo is enlarged 239% to make it into an 18x24" poster, you will have to enlarge the pages of tails to the same percentage. When the tails are printed, cut out each one and put double-sided tab on the back of each tail, at its base. Glue the poster onto a piece of foam core and prop against the wall. Blindfold each guest, hand her a tail, and point her in the direction of the poster. Winner is the person who comes closest to putting her tail at the correct spot on the poster.

Note: I'd advise printing a copyright-free photo off the Internet, as enlarging this photo into a larger image will result in an extremely fuzzy photo, hardly recognizable. Just something to think about…

Paper Telephone

You might have played the vocal form of Telephone as a kid—whispering a phrase into someone's ear, then that person whispers what he heard to a third person, and so on. At the end of the chain, the message is usually a garbled version of the original one.

In **Paper Telephone**, you will need a sheet of paper and a pen or pencil for each player. Each person begins the game by **drawing** a picture at the top of the sheet of paper. They then pass the papers to the persons to their left. These players write a **caption** below the picture and then fold the top of the papers so only the caption is showing. The papers are then passed again to the players' left. This time the players draw a **picture** that goes with the caption. The papers are folded over, leaving only the drawing exposed, and the pages are passed once again to the left. The game continues this way, alternating between drawings and captions, until every person has had a chance to make a drawing or write a caption. The papers are then unfolded and the results of drawings/captions seen. They're usually funny.

For variety, you might want to stipulate a picture/caption theme to go with the party.

Drawing – 1st person

Caption – 2nd person

Drawing – 3rd person

Caption – 4th person

Drawing – 5th person

Caption – 6th person...

Mixed Up Quotations.   Below are a few famous quotations from books and movies. They've been adapted for Groundhog's Day. Try to supply the correct quotation **and** the movie or book that the original phrase came from.

1. "You don't understand! I coulda had class. I coulda been a groundhog."

2. "All right, Mr. DeMille, I'm ready for my groundhog."

3. "Why don't you come up sometime and see my shadow?"

4. "You know how to whistle, don't you, Steve? You just put you teeth together and chatter."

5. "A boy's best friend is his groundhog."

6. "Say 'Hello' to my little shadow."

7. "Listen to them. Children of the sun. What shadows they make."

8. "I would always rather be a groundhog than dignified."

9. "Beware; for I am fearless, and therefore shadows do not alarm me."

10. "I am not afraid of sun. For I am learning how to ignore my shadow."

11. "I can't go back to my den because I was a different groundhog then."

12. "Even the darkest shadow will fade and the sun will rise."

ANSWERS to Mixed Up Quotations

1. "You don't understand! I coulda had class. I coulda been a contender." From *On the Waterfront*

2. "All right, Mr. DeMille, I'm ready for my close-up." From *Sunset Blvd.*

3. "Why don't you come up sometime and see me?" From *She Done Him Wrong*

4. "You know how to whistle, don't you, Steve? You just put you lips together and blow." From *To Have and Have Not*

5. "A boy's best friend is his mother." From *Psycho*

6. "Say 'Hello' to my little friend." From *Scarface*

7. "Listen to them. Children of the night. What music they make." From *Dracula*

8. "I would always rather be happy than dignified." From *Jane Eyre*

9. "Beware; for I am fearless, and therefore powerful." From *Frankenstein*

10. "I am not afraid of storms. For I am learning how to sail my ship." From *Little Women*

11. "I can't go back to yesterday because I was a different person then." From *Alice in Wonderland*

12. "Even the darkest night will end and the sun will rise." From *Les Miserables*

Wish Matching

Another humorous activity is **Wish Matching**. Have each person write on a piece of paper (and all paper must be identical for this so that there is no clue as to who wrote what) one thing he or she wants for this year. This item can be something tangible, like 'a set of drill bits,' or ethereal, like 'eliminate world hunger.' Have each person fold his/her paper and hand it to you. Read a wish aloud—perhaps it says 'a machete.' Then everyone will guess who in the group wishes for a machete. The person who wrote down 'a machete' will finally identify herself. Go through all the slips of paper, letting people guess who wants that thing. It is surprising to see which person wants a particular item; many times the object and the person are at extremes to what everyone guesses.

Pen and Paper Pictionary

Give a sheet of paper and a pen or pencil to each player. Everyone should write down a phrase that has to do with Groundhog's Day, then fold the paper in half. The papers are collected and put into a container. First player chooses a paper and acts out or sketches a drawing that illustrates the phrase, maybe use a large pad of newsprint paper or poster board for the drawings. The person who guesses correctly then becomes the next player to choose a paper and draw/act it out.

If you can make the phrases groundhog day themed, that would go well with the party. If not, perhaps subjects about weather or winter or spring or gardens would do well.

Mad-libs are fun. You can make up your own groundhog story or use the one supplied in this book. Either way, ask people, in turn, for the specific words *first*, then fill them in, in order, as you read the story.

Words needed for the mad-lib in this book:

A present participle: verb with an 'ing' on the end

_____

adjective _____

place _____

noun _____

famous person _____

person in the room _____

person in the room _____

person in the room _____

verb _____

person in the room _____

room or area in a house _____

Now that you have your list of words, write them in the appropriate blanks on the following page, and read the story aloud.

_____

A Groundhog's Day Tale

Groundhog's Day is here again, a time when he predicts the coming of spring. He's been (*present participle*) _____ for many months, so of course he's (*adjective*) _____ as he emerges from his (*place*) _____ . He's also hungry, so he looks around for his favorite food: (*noun*) _____ . He's got to pack on the pounds, hoping to look like (*famous person*) _____ before he goes back to sleep in October. The groundhog doesn't stray far from his den, for he runs as slow as (*person in the room*) _____ . When startled, he emits a sound very much like (*person in the room*) _____ singing. Never try to calm a frightened groundhog by picking him up. Instead, show him a photo of (*person in room*) _____ and he will (*verb*) _____ . Although groundhogs like to live in meadows and along the fringe of woods, there are recorded sightings in (*person in the room*) _____ 's (*room or area in a house*) _____ .

Of course you will want to sing Groundhog Day carols! Isn't this why you bought this book?

Whatever you do, however you decorate, whether you have a buffet or snacks or a proper meal, your party will be memorable. Have fun!

Immerse yourself in the McLaren mystery!

Listen to the songs that are important to the victim and the story!

Single-song CDs recorded by
St. Louis-area musicians in a variety of styles, from
folk, blues, jug band, Handel aria, classic jazz, and
an original composition for 2-pianos.

Available from the author's website
www.johiestand.com.

A conversation with Jo and Rusty

Question:	Jo, you've written carols for Groundhog's Day. This sparks a lot of questions, but the first is: why Groundhog's Day and not, for instance, Christmas or Thanksgiving?
Jo:	Several reasons: first of all, to my knowledge there aren't many songs for Groundhog's Day! The holiday is woefully overlooked in that regard. Second, I've had groundhogs in my back yard for years. I think they're cute and I love watching them. My affinity for them just evolved into making up song parodies about them.
Question:	Have you written other songs?
Jo:	Lyrics, only. Those are for the companion songs to the McLaren mysteries that I write. Although I'm fairly musical—I play the harpsichord and guitar, I've been a member of a folk singing group—I don't really write much.
Question:	You just mentioned having groundhogs in your back yard.... Did you entice them there or do you live in a rural area where they are common?
Jo:	I live in St Louis county, of all places! But there's a creek that borders my back yard, and I have a stand of trees, too. A perfect habitat for groundhogs. They were living there when I moved in. I saw one at the back of my property one day—I remember thinking it was a beaver at first because I saw just a glimpse of its head. But of course

the tail gave it away as being a groundhog. Anyway, I started leaving food on my back deck, hoping to entice it to a closer viewing range for me. It worked, and ever since I've had a succession of groundhogs chomping merrily away through the spring, summer and fall months.

Question: What do you leave out for them?

Jo: Certainly, vegetables. Nearly everything: tomatoes, carrots, broccoli, strawberries, melons—they *love* melons!

Rusty: Cantaloupe....yum. And honeydew...and peaches....

Jo: Zucchini, corn on the cob.... Nuts and seeds, of course. They munch on the spilled seed from the bird feeders. And something that most people would not even think of: baked goods. Muffins, cookies, graham crackers, bread, bagels.

Question: Baked goods! Did you know they like that, or was this some odd discovery?

Jo: I put out bread and crackers and such for the raccoons and possums. I knew they loved that. But some were left over one night and I just happened to see the groundhog eat it. Rather enthusiastically, I might add! He (or she...I can't tell their gender) preferred that to his (or her) veggies!

Rusty: We aren't dumb. We gnaw what we like!

Question: Anything they don't like?

Rusty: Fooey on potatoes.

Jo: Sometimes I put out a salt block. Groundhogs need salt in their diet, as do many animals. In fact, you can see groundhogs in the early spring at the edges of roads, licking up the salt that's put down to rid the roads of ice and snow.

Question: Really?

Rusty: This and more fun facts are in her book. We're an interesting animal!

Question: Sounds like this keeps you busy, Jo, feeding your wild life menagerie.

Jo: I put out the food for the groundhogs early in the morning, then sometimes late in the afternoon, depending on how many groundhogs I have in a particular year. Right now I have two who habituate my deck. I put out food for the possums and the raccoons in the early evening. Birds get fed, too, but that's it.

Question: You don't try to make pets of these animals, do you?

Jo: No! I would never do that. Wild animals should stay wild.

Rusty: Besides, our daily routines would clash…

Question: Yet you are, in a sense, treating them like pets, making them dependent on you for food.

Jo: Believe me, I don't feed them enough to make them dependent. I don't supply their entire daily portion. I just put out a bit of food so they come onto my deck to eat, which lets me watch them, photograph them, and learn a bit about each species. They wander away and then forage for the rest of their meal on their own. I'm just trying to help them survive in an ever-encroaching urban environment. These animals have as much right to life, a safe place to live, and plentiful food as we have. Human beings don't own the earth.

Question: Well, Jo, you sound as though you know a bit about these animals. Will you write another book on groundhogs?

Rusty: We're trying to persuade her to do a coffee table photo book on us, but so far we haven't seen a shadow of a draft.

Author Jo A. Hiestand

Jo A. Hiestand encountered her first groundhog in 1997 when she moved into her new house. Humphrey promptly introduced himself and made himself at home when Jo started feeding him on the back deck. Since then her back yard has seen many groundhogs: Montgomery, Winston, Toby, and Rusty, to name a few. She's learned a lot about them and the foods they love to eat, which includes muffins! A book on Groundhog's Day carols was certain to evolve, a natural combination of her years of observations and love of music.

Perhaps on a more serious side, she is also the author of two Derbyshire-based mystery series. The Taylor & Graham series uses British customs as the backbone of each book's plot. The McLaren Mysteries feature ex-police detective Michael McLaren, who investigates cold cases on his own. Her cookbook, *Cider, Swords and Straw*, is a companion piece to the Taylor & Graham novels, and features over three hundred recipes based on the customs highlighted in the plots.

Jo's insistence for accuracy—from police methods and location layout to the general "feel" of the area—has driven her innumerable times to Derbyshire, England, the setting for her books.   These explorations and conferences with police friends provide the details in the novels.

She has combined her love of writing, board games and music by co-inventing *P.I.R.A.T.E.S.*, the mystery-solving game that uses maps, graphics, song lyrics, and other clues to lead the players to the lost treasure.

In 2001 Jo graduated from Webster University with a BA degree in English and departmental honors.

Jo founded the Greater St. Louis Chapter of Sisters in Crime, serving as its first president.

Her cat, Tennyson, shares her St. Louis home.

ଛଠ

For more information about Jo, or to keep up to date with new book information, scheduled talks and signings, visit her on the web at www.johiestand.com

If you enjoyed the recipes in this book, check out the more than 300 recipes in the Taylor & Graham companion cookbook *Cider, Swords and Straw*! Available from Amazon.com, barnesandnoble.com, iBooks.com, Kobo.com, and overdrive.com

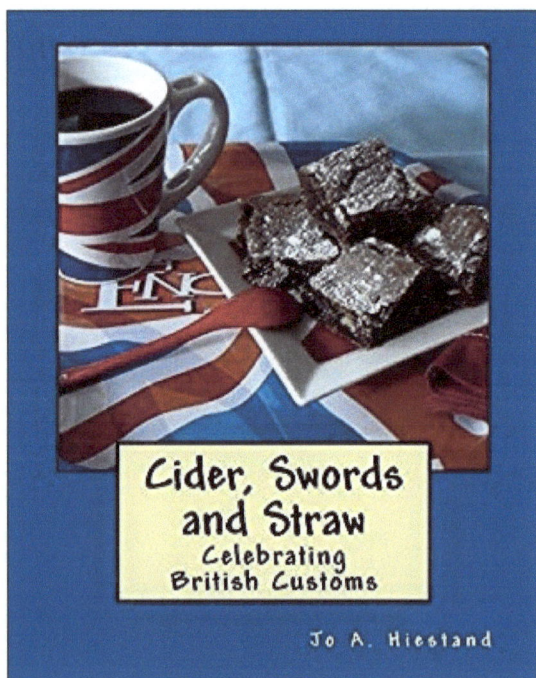

Cider, Swords and Straw
Celebrating British Customs

Jo A. Hiestand

www.ingramcontent.com/pod-product-compliance
Lightning Source LLC
Chambersburg PA
CBHW041358090426
42741CB00001B/3